YOUR KNOWLEDGE HAS VALUE

Bibliographic information published by the German National Library:

The German National Library lists this publication in the National Bibliography;
detailed bibliographic data are available on the Internet at http://dnb.dnb.de .

Imprint:

Copyright © 2002 GRIN Verlag, Open Publishing GmbH
Print and binding: Books on Demand GmbH, Norderstedt Germany
ISBN: 9783668121881

This book at GRIN:

http://www.grin.com/en/e-book/138137/a-short-examination-of-haunani-kay-trask-
s-settlers-of-color-and-immigrant

Stephanie Wössner

A short examination of Haunani-Kay Trask's "Settlers of Color and 'Immigrant' Hegemony: 'Locals' in Hawai'i"

GRIN Publishing

GRIN - Your knowledge has value

Since its foundation in 1998, GRIN has specialized in publishing academic texts by students, college teachers and other academics as e-book and printed book. The website www.grin.com is an ideal platform for presenting term papers, final papers, scientific essays, dissertations and specialist books.

Visit us on the internet:

http://www.grin.com/

http://www.facebook.com/grincom

http://www.twitter.com/grin_com

I INTRODUCTION 2

1. The author 2

2. The article 2

II MAIN PART 4

1. What is the central theme / statement of the article ? 4

a. Why is this topic of any value ?..4

b. Why did you choose to critically analyze this article ? 4

2. What methods does the author use to achieve their stated conclusions or results ?...5

a. Are those methods likely to produce accurate data ? 6

b. What are the indicated or inferred perspectives or biases of the writer ? 6

3. What did you learn from the article ?...6

a. What are its most important statements or conclusions ?...................................7

b. Are there any significant weaknesses in any statements, major or supportive ? Is the article logically sound ?...7

c. Does the article agree or conflict with your own personal views ? How and why ?...........9

d. Does the article contribute significantly to the general body of knowledge about Asian Americans ?...9

4. Could this work be improved ? 10

a. What logical basis is there for changes that you would make ?........................10

b. Would your changes produce significantly or substantially different results ? Why ? 11

III CONCLUSION 12

I INTRODUCTION

1. The author

Holder of a Ph.D degree in political science from the University of Wisconsin, Dr. Haunani Kay-Trask is presently a professor of Hawaiian Studies at the University of Hawai'i. As one of the founders and core members of Ka Lāhui Hawai'i, the largest Hawaiian organization for native sovereignty, she has represented Hawai'i's indigenous people at many indigenous meetings around the world. She has also published many articles on the Hawaiian struggle for self-determination. Besides her teaching and political career, Dr. Trask is also a widely published poets and writer. Among her publications is the book *From a Native Daughter: Colonialism and Sovereignty in Hawai'i.* [1]

2. The article

"Settlers of Color and 'Immigrant' Hegemony: 'Locals' in Hawai'i" was published in *Amerasia Journal 26:2* (summer 2000). This was a special issue dedicated to the question "Whose Vision ?: Asian Settler Colonialism in Hawai'i."

The article constitutes an advocacy of Native Hawaiian sovereignty and talks about the growing tensions between Asians and Native Hawaiians in Hawai'i. Trask believes that settler organizations, such as the JACL, intentionally obscure the issue of justice for Hawaiians by stirring up hatred against native leaders. She bases her analysis of the question of Asian/Japanese "alleged support" of the sovereignty movement on the JACL's reaction to her sister Mililani Trask's claim that Senator Daniel Inouye controlled the sovereignty process by giving available funds only to his favorites, who are against Native

---

[1] http://www.unescocat.org/Haunani.html

Hawaiian sovereignty. The JACL, the Democratic Party, and the Honolulu dailies, so Trask, teamed up to attack her sister back, thereby obscuring her whole analysis of the real issue. Opponents of Hawaiian sovereignty accuse Native Hawaiians of "going down the race road," but Trask believes that this is just a means of hiding the real race issue, namely the Japanese's desire to keep their power. She describes Asian success as the "latest elaboration of foreign hegemony," and says that Hawaiians remain a politically subordinated group. They are believed to be inassimilable and a "failed indigenous people." According to her, those in power deny Native Hawaiian claims through the ideology of "power sharing," which makes Native Hawaiians one of many ethnic groups of the islands. Having been robbed all their power, they basically have nothing left to share and those in power feel they have earned their dominant position. During the 1990s, anti-Hawaiian sentiments have emerged among both the *haole* (whites) and Asians. This is, according to Trask, a response to an old sovereignty movement among Hawaiians for self government. In an attempt to set themselves apart from the *haole*, Asians claim a "local nation" in Hawai'i. This settler claim is a fictitious socio-political entity to justify non-Native hegemony and to hide the fact that Asians have risen in social status through the oppression of Native Hawaiians by the white colonizers. Trask holds the opinion that Hawaiians have to start a de-colonization – both politically and mentally – by reconnecting themselves to their nation. Their fight is for national liberation and not merely a kind of identity politics. American nationality has to be rejected, their lands and resources have to be restored, self-determination and a nation-to-nation relationship with the United States have to be established. The determining voice has to be Native Hawaiian, even if support by non-Hawaiians is desirable.

II MAIN PART

1. What is the central theme / statement of the article ?

As the title already indicates, the central theme of the article are the Asian immigrants who call themselves "locals" and who want to establish their own nation in Hawai'i, a nation separate from the white colonizers. Trask states that these Asians oppose the Native Hawaiian struggle for self-determination because they do not want to give up the power they presently hold on the islands. She uses these reflection to passionately advocate Native Hawaiian sovereignty.

a. Why is this topic of any value ?

The value of this topic lies, first of all, in its illustration of the positionality of Asians in Hawai'i. Contrary to the mainland, Asians in Hawai'i, currently about 41 % of the total population, are beneficiaries of the structure and part of the system. Nevertheless, they do not want to identify with the white elite. Moreover, this article shows the oppression of Native Hawaiians, the injustices committed against them, and their fight for national liberation. This oppression of Native Hawaiians is a late effect of US colonialism, imperialism and capitalism. Finally, Trask depicts the racial dynamics of present-day Hawai'i.

b. Why did you choose to critically analyze this article ?

I chose this article because it portrays the differences between the situation of mainland Asian Americans and Asian Americans living in Hawai'i. My main interest in Asian American Studies lies in the study of Japanese Americans, and since Japanese Americans constitute, at present, the biggest Asian ethnic group on the islands, I thought this article would also give me some more insights in differences within the diverse group called Japanese Americans. What also appealed to me was the fact that the article was written by a nationalist. Her thesis seemed very powerful to me but once I had finished reading the article for the first time, I felt compelled to go over it again to find out why I was not completely satisfied with her way of proving it.

2. What methods does the author use to achieve their stated conclusions or results ?

Trask uses different methods in proving her point of view on national sovereignty and the relationship between Asians and Native Hawaiians. In her advocacy of national sovereignty, she recapitulates the history of colonization that led to the disempowerment of Native Hawaiians and the present situation. She then compares this situation to the political changes as far as indigenous peoples are concerned and makes clear that this political framework has to be applied to Native Hawaiians as well. She refers, among others, to the UN Charter on equal rights and self-determination of peoples and to the Draft Declaration on the Rights of Indigenous Peoples. She also sums up different studies conducted to define the terms "peoples" and "minorities" in order to make sure everyone understands that Native Hawaiians are not a minority. She then turns to the Ka Lāhui Master Plan which states the goals of Native Hawaiian political action. The Master Plan serves as an illustration of the distance between Native Hawaiians and "locals" as it contrasts the ideal and real state of power relations in Hawai'i.

As far as the tensions between Asians and Native Hawaiians are concerned, Trask talks about the reaction of the Democratic Party and the JACL when her sister Mililani Trask accused Senator Daniel Inouye of hindering the strive for national liberation and sovereignty.

a. Are those methods likely to produce accurate data ?

The historical background, despite the fact that history can be interpreted in many different ways, should be a strong argument to justify the struggle for Native Hawaiian sovereignty, especially since it is backed up by recent political developments. However, using the story of a family member to illustrate the tensions between Asians and Native Hawaiians may not have been the best choice. After a fairly objective reiteration of facts, she starts to get emotional and angry and to personally attack Senator Inouye and the JACL. Her feelings are of course understandable but I think they render her arguments less powerful.

b. What are the indicated or inferred perspectives or biases of the writer ?

It is very obvious that the author is a devoted Native Hawaiian nationalist and that this nationalistic attitude makes her, at times, abandon her objectivity.

3. What did you learn from the article ?

Although I already knew about the sovereignty movement in Hawai'i and about the quite different position of Asians on the islands, it was very insightful to hear an insider's perspective. Before reading the article, as biased as it may be in certain aspects, I did not now anything about the degree of disputes between Native Hawaiians and Asians,the Democratic Party and Senator Inouye. I was also not aware of the role of the JACL in Hawai'i.

a. What are its most important statements or conclusions ?

In my opinion, there are several important statements and conclusions in the article worth mentioning. Number one, Asians are called the latest foreign hegemony which basically places them on the same level with the white colonizers. Number two, Trask explains that there is an intra-settler conflict with Asians setting themselves apart from the *haole*, just as they set themselves apart from the indigenous population. Number three, she claims that Asians, especially the Japanese, call for a "local nation" because they do not want to cede the power they presently have, and that they want to obscure the fact that their position is due to oppression of Native Hawaiians. Number four, Trask promotes national sovereignty and Native Hawaiian self-determination. Number five, she stresses the necessity of support of their cause by "serious and thoughtful individuals" of non-Native origin. Number six, the situation of Native Hawaiians is compared to that of Native Americans. The latter have already established self-government and a nation-to-nation relationship with the United States, so Native Hawaiians sovereignty should follow. Number seven, Trask calls the Ka Lāhui Master Plan the "clearest document in Hawaiian history" and declares those non-Natives who support the struggle for Hawaiian sovereignty supporters of all struggles of indigenous peoples which created the Draft Declaration.

Finally, there is one conclusion that can be inferred from the description of Asian behavior on the islands, namely that Asians on the islands behave in many ways like those white Americans who wanted to exclude Asians on the mainland.

b. Are there any significant weaknesses in any statements, major or supportive ? Is the article logically sound ?

There are two points that I believe to be pretty weak in supporting the main statements of the article, especially the fact that the Japanese do not want to give up their power. On the

one hand, Trask does not make any effort to back up her interpretation of the dispute

between her sister and the JACL with external arguments. She only sees it from her

personal point of view which seems to be very subjective and emotional. On the other hand,

there is an inconsistency in her reasoning concerning Asians in Hawai'i. At the beginning of

the article she uses the term "Asian" all the time but once she gets into her personal

crusade against the JACL and Senator Inouye she picks only on the Japanese. Although it

is true that Japanese Americans constitute the largest ethnic group of all Asians (16.7 % in

2000^2), there are other groups making up the remaining 24.9 % of the Asian population.

The largest of these remaining groups are Filipinos with 14.1 %[2]. Also, she speaks about

the Japanese as if they were a homogenous and pure ethnic group. Looking at the great

number (21.4 %) of *hapa* persons in Hawai'i, it is very probable that not all Japanese are of

100 % Japanese origin. There are also Okinawan folks on the islands, who may be viewed

by some people as Japanese. My only guess as to why she constantly picks on the

Japanese is the influential position Senator Inouye and the JACL hold. Finally, her

statements are sometimes a little too encompassing, so one could easily get the

impression all Japanese, or all Asians are against Native Hawaiian sovereignty. Even

though she mentions that there are some supporters of their cause among the non-Natives,

this statement is not really stressed throughout the article.

I would say that the article is logically pretty sound regarding Trask's advocacy of

sovereignty, but that it is less logical when Trask's personal attitudes and anger interfere.

---

[2]http://factfinder.census.gov/servlet/BasicFactsTable?_lang=en&_vt_name=DEC_2000_SF1_U_DP1&_geo_id=04000US15

c. Does the article agree or conflict with your own personal views ? How and why ?

I agree with Trask that independence on Native Hawaiian terms is the only way to restore all the wrongs that have been done in the past. That she seems to advocate only relatively peaceful actions has my absolute approval. I also agree with her that those non-Natives who are aware of the reality should help fight alongside Native Hawaiians for national liberation and that education in history and culture of Hawai'i may be a starting point to de-colonize the mind. However, I would suggest she not lose out of sight the fact that Asians are not responsible for the colonization of their Native land but that white Americans are. She also should not forget that Asians, socialized in schools in Hawai'i, are taught to be the way they are, so she might consider to also try and educate Asians, maybe even advocate a change in the educational system.

d. Does the article contribute significantly to the general body of knowledge about Asian Americans ?

Despite the anger inherent in a couple of passages, the article *does* contribute to the general body of knowledge about Asian Americans. The reader is presented an inside view on Hawaiian sovereignty, and he clearly sees in what aspects the situation of Asians in Hawai'i is different from those on the mainland. The consequences of US colonialism, imperialism, and capitalism are also very efficiently depicted. And despite the personal and angry undertone in her attack on Japanese Americans, what Trask says about the role of the Japanese on the islands is not made up either. In my opinion, this is one of the main contributions to the knowledge about Asian Americans, for we hear a lot more about mainland Japanese Americans and issues concerning them (such as the redress movement for example).

4. Could this work be improved ?

There are actually a couple of points I would improve. These suggestions are based on my personal point of view, on my limited knowledge, and I certainly do not claim to tell the ultimate truth. First of all, I would leave out the personal attack against the JACL and Japanese Americans after the recounting of the controversy between Mililani Trask and the JACL. Second, I am not sure if it makes sense to use a premordialist, or essentialist, approach to the category of Native Hawaiians. After all, this is not a homogenous group at all. For example, it does not take into account hybridity, i.e. the fact that many of the so called Native Hawaiians are actually *hapa*, i.e. half-Native Hawaiian, half-other. She also does not mention Asian groups other than Japanese or persons of mixed heritage within the Japanese community. What Trask leaves out as well is the reaction of other non-Asian ethnic groups in Hawai'i, such as American Indians, African Americans, and Latinos. As far as terminology is concerned, the use of the term "settler" for Asians in Hawai'i is a little bit problematic, for it is usually used in colonial contexts. In this case however, the "settlers" come from a different country than the colonizer. When talking about the term "local," Trask usually associates it with an Asian version of the Horatio Alger story, whereas she does not mention that this term was used as a political term in the 1970s, when non-Natives wanted to show their ties to the land of Native Hawaiians. Finally, as I have already mentioned, Trask's rhetoric of anger may not be the right way to convince a scholarly audience of her views.

a. What logical basis is there for changes that you would make ?

The changes I suggest would make the part of the article trying to explain the tensions between Asians and Native Hawaiians more convincing in that it would leave out any personal feelings of anger. The substitution of the term "settler" for a more appropriate designation would prevent the article as a whole from being discredited in case someone is familiar with the exact meaning of the term "settler." (Nevertheless, I am aware of the fact that the article was published in a collection of essays under the title "Asian Settler Colonialism in Hawai'i" which may have caused the use of the term.) Finally, by including groups other than the Japanese, including persons of mixed heritage and other racial groups, the article would reflect the diversity of Hawai'i a lot more accurately.

b. Would your changes produce significantly or substantially different results ? Why ?

Yes, I believe that my changes would produce different results in that the nationalistic undertone would be less powerful but the arguments would possibly be more convincing for a scholarly/intellectual audience. My suggested inclusion of other ethnic and racial, as well as mixed ethnic/racial individuals and groups would make the picture of Hawai'i more complete and accurate. However, such an inclusion might also have the consequence of presenting a too diverse and confusing picture of the situation. Especially by including mixed ethnic/racial individuals and making clear that there are very few "pure" Native Hawaiians, one could come to the conclusion that the strife for sovereignty is not justified. This inclusion would also render the thesis of tension between Asians/the Japanese and Native Hawaiians less convincing because "the Japanese" would suddenly be divided into many small groups.

III CONCLUSION

Even though this article is written from a very nationalistic point of view and has its weaknesses, the anger Trask expresses is very understandable if we consider the history of oppression her people has had to endure. She cannot be blamed for her passionate advocacy of Native Hawaiian sovereignty. Despite her passion, she should, however, try not to lose out of sight reality as it is. At some points in her article she seemed a little bit too idealistic in her aims. I do not say that idealism should be abandoned, for it is exactly this idealism which can make the world change, but sometimes we should take a step back and look at everything objectively in order not to seek the impossible, in order to find ways to get massive support from outside our group for our own cause.